# PROPHETICALLY SPEAKING...

## TODAY IS A NEW DAY

CAROLYN KING-ROBERTSON

LOVE CLONES

*publishing*

Love Clones Publishing
www.lcpublishing.net

ISBN: 978-0692564837

Publishers:
Love Clones Publishing
Dallas, TX 75025
www.lcpublishing.net

# DEDICATION

This book is dedicated to all the men and women
who have been bruised in spirit, hurt by the spirit
of religious practice and tradition as well as those
who has or are experiencing backlash as you begin
to walk in your purpose in the earth.

# THANK YOU'S

I would like to thank first the Trinity, The Father, The Son & The Holy Ghost, for keeping me, saving me, leading and teaching me through this journey of greater. Thank you to my husband, children and grandchildren Joshua, Jeremiah and Makhi who inspired me even at such a young age to push forward in all that God has for me and to leave a legacy for them. My parents Charles & Sheila Bagley, my grandmother Beulah R King,

To my Pastor David L Norman and Chief Apostle C Kevin & Apostle Candace N Ford. I am grateful to all my family and friends for your prayers, encouragement, love and support.

Thank You!!

CAROLYN KING-ROBERTSON

# PROPHETICALLY SPEAKING...

## TODAY IS A NEW DAY

# DAY 1

*Jesus Christ has already given us an identity.*

I will no longer wait for anyone to acknowledge me as a champion. I know who I am and pleasing man will no longer exist in my thought process. I declare that I am already victorious

> *But Thanks be to God. He gives us the victory though our Lord Jesus Christ.*
> *-1 Corinthians 15:57 (NIV)*

**Today is a New Day!**

Today I declare:

_____

_____

_____

_____

_____

_____

Prayer:   Father thank you for claiming me as your own; the apple of your eye. A diamond that was cut from a different cloth, specifically for your use in the earth. Thank you for reminding me Holy Spirit that I walk in victory because Jesus Christ paid the price in full and the balance is zero because of Him.

# DAY 2

The mind is like a website. If it was to access a contaminated link, it becomes toxic, containing a number of viruses. Be mindful of your connections. Some past connections carry a bug that will destroy your future if not detected in time.

I declare that my connections are divine and strategically planned by God. I release relationships God has instructed me to release.

**Today is a new day!**

Today I declare:

_____

_____

_____

_____

_____

_____

Prayer: Father, help me to be mindful of who I am opening myself up to in this season. Amen

# DAY 3

Dead weight has a tendency to hold us back. Therefore, In order to grasp hold of new beginnings, inactive people, places and things have to be done away with if we expect movement to occur.

Today I Declare that anything that is dead in my life but God has said it should live, will be filled with purpose and I will

_____

_____

**Today is a new day!**

Prayer: Father, help me let go of any hindrances that are keeping me from moving forward and growing. Remind me that as I advance and grow, those who you have sent to me will have an opportunity to advance and grow as well. Remind me daily that it is not about me. Amen

Today I declare:

_____

_____

_____

_____

_____

_____

# DAY 4

Setbacks are sometimes setups to position us in a proper place of alignment with the order of God. There is a difference between encountering setbacks caused by our own delays of procrastination verses those, which are planned by God. When God is at work, I prefer to view the set back as my molding season or perhaps a season of preparation, a season of character building, or a season of growth.

The setback can also be a "setup" orchestrated by God to protect us from a disaster ahead. God knows all things. The omniscience of God is that our future is secure. Not because we know what lies ahead but simply because God knows.

The Word of God tells us that Joseph's brothers sold him into slavery but told their father a wild animal killed him. He was falsely accused of attacking Potiphar's wife, thrown into prison but

God even then was setting him up for greatness as Joseph remained faithful and obedient to God. (Genesis 37,39)

**Today is a new day!**

Prayer: Holy Spirit, help me to recognize when God has ordained the setback or when I have caused my own chaos.  Take me to that place of repentance that will allow me to position myself back in alignment with the Father and GET TO WORK!  Give me strength to press on in a way that honors you even when it seems all odds are against me. Amen

Today I declare:

_____

_____

_____

_____

_____

_____

# DAY 5

The mouth sprouts out much, however the weight behind it carries very little impact if we are known to be unreliable in any situation. It is vain speaking before God to never finish what we have begun or never beginning what we have committed to start. In all that we commit to doing, it must be done to the glory of God.

"Commit to the Lord whatever you do and all your plans will succeed." Proverbs 16:3 (NIV)

**Today is a new day!**

Today I declare:

_____

_____

_____

_____

_____

_____

Prayer: Father, teach me to honor my word when given. Help me to refrain from saying yes to whatever will cause me to become overwhelmed with self-appointed assignments.

Holy Spirit I invite you in to show me which assignments to say yes to and remind me that saying "NO" is necessary sometimes.

# DAY 6

Abandonment of good character strips the true anointing. We cannot confuse the people by sending mixed signals

We are ambassadors of Jesus Christ and should act accordingly. Our anointing alone will only take us but so far. Bad character is an anointing killer. We can be full in our anointing yet foolish in our ways

**Today is a new day!**

Today I declare:

_____

_____

_____

_____

_____

_____

Prayer: Father, remind me today that my anointing is a gift from You. A gift I have received by grace but know I don't deserve. Holy Spirit, give me the words to say in every situation so that I may respond only when you have released me to do so and in a way that pleases the Father. Help me to continue to walk and operate through the light of Jesus Christ, putting away any and all self absorbing emotions whether through words, actions or thoughts. Amen

# Day 7

Attention to detail and actions that follow will give insight in many situations. (Discern)

Some people are still trying to be playmates instead of real prayer partners, teachers, encouragers, supporters, true servants and vessels of God.

"Watch out for false prophets. They come to you in sheep's clothing but inwardly they are ferocious wolves." Matthew 7:15 ( NIV )

Be careful of who you open yourself up to. True men and women of God will act accordingly and not lustfully or self-seeking for vain glory in any manner.

**Today is a new day!**

Today I declare:

_____

_____

_____

_____

_____

_____

Prayer: Father help me to recognize those men and women of God you are sending my way and let me discern those who may have their own personal agenda. Remove any blinders that may try to blurry my eyes or unnecessary noise in my ears that will keep me from seeing and hearing clearly from you! Activate my spirit of discernment in greater portion, so I may see and hear in the spirit realm what is happening in the natural. Amen

# DAY 8

When we are obedient to God, He opens and closes doors. Closed doors do not always suggest the end of your purpose. It just means that it was not the door God wanted you to walk through. Take heed to His instructions and plant His word in your spirit. What God has for you is specifically for you. Do not give up!

**Today is a new day!**

Prayer: Father thank you for being so mindful of me that you would keep me from what is not for me and making me secure and safe in what is. You are an awesome God! Amen

Today I declare:

_____

_____

_____

_____

_____

_____

# DAY 9

People pleasers and people chasers will always come up short. Obedience to man with no thought and sincerity of obedience to God blocks our blessings and hinders our prayers. It is also a spirit of rebellion in operation.

What has God shown you about you in your Spirit? When God has instructed us to carry out a particular assignment (s) are we more concerned with the voice of man rather than the instructions given to us by God? Are we busy chasing after big names and large man made thing's instead of pursuing what is on the heart of God completely!

Are we so determined to have our name called in the church that we are willing to sell God out by becoming pulpit puppets and a dictated congregational crew for man?!
Father, show me myself in regards to my obedience towards you.

Let us pause right here! If we have found ourselves to have fallen in this trap in even the smallest of ways, repentance is now!

Thank You Father for your forgiveness. I can now move on in the plans you have ordained for my life.

If we confess our sins, He is faithful and just to forgive us of our sins and to cleanse us from all unrighteousness. 1 John 1:9 (KJV)

**Today is a new day!**

Today I declare:

_____

_____

_____

_____

_____

# Day 10

When our struggles and circumstances are great in measure it is the power of God that rises up in us and gives us strength to endure

Father regardless of any situation I face today, I call on you El Shaddai, God Almighty the all sufficient God who gives me nourishment in every part of my being. I will be strengthened through today's journey because I know you cover and keep me every step of the way.

Do not be afraid, you who are highly esteemed," he said. "Peace! Be strong now; be strong." When he spoke to me, I was strengthened and said, "Speak, my lord, since you have given me strength." Daniel 10:19 (NIV)

**Today is a new day!**

Today I declare:

_____

_____

_____

_____

_____

_____

# DAY 11

Determination and motivation have to be active in our DNA. Think about it! If we say we are the seed of Abraham then we know that he was not lazy and he obeyed God seeking to do His will. We have an inheritance but we also have assignments and a purpose in the earth to fulfill.

Today I will be fully charged by the grace of God to do the work and not just dream about it or talk about it. Today I am expecting the promises of God to come to pass as I hold up my end as the seed of Abraham

And now that you belong to Christ, you are the true children of Abraham. You are his heirs, and God's promise to Abraham belongs to you.
Galatians 3:29 ( NLT )

**Today is a new day!**

Today I declare:

_____

_____

_____

_____

_____

_____

# Day 12

Mind Management is just as important as time management. If our mind and our thoughts are all over the place, it will be very difficult to actually focus on what we need to be spending time on. Today, challenge yourself to manage (discern ) what comes into thought, what takes residence and what should be booted out. No time to waste. The clock does not stop simply because we allow our mind or train of thought to become distracted by  foolishness

Colossians 3:1-2 (NASB ) Therefore if you have been raised up with Christ, keep seeking the things above, where Christ is, seated at the right hand of God. Set your mind on the things above, not on the things that are on the earth

**Today is a new day!**

Today I declare:

_____

_____

_____

_____

_____

_____

# DAY 13

Our flesh and our spirit man cannot walk together and still be effective in leading souls to Christ. Our spirit man has to overpower our flesh constantly. Often times some of us get confused in our thinking that we are exempt from circumstances in life, things and people. It is truly amazing how we as Christians react in some cases where it is difficult to even see that we are children of God. I guess some have not figured out that the enemy has an assignment for their lives as well. Yet you must not employ him. Fire him and all his assistants. Move by the leading of the Holy Spirit in everything. Declare, Holy Spirit, activate yourself in me today.

Romans 8:5 ( NLT ) Those who are dominated by the sinful nature think about sinful things, but those who are controlled by the Holy Spirit think about things that please the Spirit.

# Today is a new day!

Today I declare:

_____

_____

_____

_____

_____

_____

# DAY 14

New mindset and old behavior and ideas will eventually bump heads. WHY? Because the old person we use to be would rather remain in comfort instead of thinking Kingdom. If our train of thought is always on "use to be " it leaves no room for the "new" of what is to come all the while destroying the vision of great expectations and witnessing the manifestation in full effect.

Mark 2:22 ( NIV)  And no one pours new wine into old wineskins. Otherwise, the wine will burst the skins, and both the wine and the wineskins will be ruined. No, they pour new wine into new wineskins."

Today I lay to rest for good anything old and stale that is lingering on in me of "use to be" so I can move forward in my new beginnings with a new mindset.  Fresh oil!

## Today is a new day!

Today I declare:

_____

_____

_____

_____

_____

_____

# DAY 15

Dream killers and fake friends do exist. Check your connections. We cannot be so desperate to be connected or remain connected with people that we forget to seek counsel from the Holy Spirit. Those who you are connected with should be those who believe in you, support and encourage you, even if they are not in your presence. Make sure they are not firing darts at you in secret while appearing to be supportive in public.

Proverbs 27:17 ( NIV) As iron sharpens iron, so one person sharpens another

Father, open my eyes today that I may see what you are desiring for me to see, not just in other's but in me as well

**Today is a new day!**

Today I declare:

_____

_____

_____

_____

_____

_____

# DAY 16

ICS: Identity Crisis Syndrome - never allow anyone to freely strip you from who God purposed you to be just to create another one of themselves. Know who you are in Him in your new journey and not from what others may label you according to your past history.

Galatians 2:20 (NLT)  My old self has been crucified with Christ. It is no longer I who live, but Christ lives in me. So I live in this earthly body by trusting in the Son of God, who loved me and gave himself for me.

Father today I am a new creature because of your Son Jesus Christ, not prideful but humbled with an entirely new address in my supernatural journey with you!

# Today is a new day!

Today I declare:

_____

_____

_____

_____

_____

_____

# DAY 17

Your life has a purpose, live it to your fullest potential. Watch out for too much familiarity and comfort which can potentially keep you productive but never producing.

Purpose: the reason for which something is done or created or for which something exist

Producing: To bring forth

Genesis 9:7 (ESV) And you, be fruitful and multiply, increase greatly on the earth and multiply in it.

Father today show me how to do your bidding through every gift you have blessed me with to plant good seeds that will multiply abundantly and bring glory and honor to your name

**Today is a new day!**

Today I declare:

_____

_____

_____

_____

_____

_____

# DAY 18

Did you know that hell is a one-way ticket and a refund policy does not exist. The reality is, we cannot go through life living as if we will be here on earth forever. We have to grow up at some point and choose Christ permanently and not on a temporary basis.

Galatians 6:8 ( NIV ) Whoever sows to please their flesh, from the flesh will reap destruction; whoever sows to please the Spirit, from the Spirit will reap eternal life.

Today is a new day and I will not waste another minute crucifying my Saviour all over again because of the desires of my flesh

Today I declare:

_____

_____

_____

_____

_____

_____

# DAY 19

Find your place in the Lord and He will assign you your place in the earth. Live life unsurprised on purpose, prepared to do the will of the Father without compromise. It's that simple!

1 Cor 7:17 (ESV) Only let each person lead the life that the Lord has assigned to him, and to which God has called him. This is my rule in all the churches.

**Today is a new day!**

Today I declare:

_____

_____

_____

_____

_____

_____

# DAY 20

God will not leave us where we are unless we choose to remain there. We minimize choice to the point seemingly as if it is not an option to us. It is our choice if we decide to move on or remain stagnant, being confined, motionless, no activity, depressed, sluggish, or inactive. There is always hope in Jesus Christ when we choose to trust Him.

Psalm 55:22 (NIV) Cast your cares on the LORD and he will sustain you; he will never let the righteous be shaken.

Lord I put my trust in you. I lay it all at your feet

Today I choose to turn over a new leaf and view my life as one that does matter and trust God for the outcome in all things. Father I choose you.

**Today is a new day!**

Today I declare:

_____

_____

_____

_____

_____

_____

# DAY 21

The Word of God speaks of blessings but it also speaks of repentance and correction. Beware of those who only speak of the blessings while standing on the sidelines watching many slipping and sliding back and forth in the ways of the world. Beware of false prophets.

1 John:1 (NLT) Dear friends, do not believe everyone who claims to speak by the Spirit. You must test them to see if the spirit they have comes from God. For there are many false prophets in the world.

Lord, teach me to discern those you send as oppose to those who come but have not been sent by you.

**Today is a new day!**

Today I declare:

_____

_____

_____

_____

_____

_____

# DAY 22

I am forgiven.

Release past failures and those who have made it their number one priority to keep reminding you of them. You may be overdue for a change of scenery.

Blessed are those whose disobedience is forgiven and whose sins are pardoned. Romans 4:7 (GWT)

**Today is a new day!**

Today I declare:

_____

_____

_____

_____

_____

_____

# DAY 23

The carnal mind says take the short cut, the easy route in everything. If we are not willing to take the journey head on, exactly the way God intended us too, we find ourselves in a place of disobedience and a journey full of chaos and confusion. The absence of peace is inevitable.

Listen to my instruction and be wise. Don't ignore it. Proverbs 8:33 (NLT)

Lord, help me not to cheat on this journey but to travel it the exact way it has been predestined for me

**Today is a new day!**

Today I declare:

_____

_____

_____

_____

_____

_____

# DAY 24

What we view as an ending may be a beginning in the sight of God. Embrace the journey! Have faith in knowing that as He spoke in the beginning of time and created all things, he also spoke our destiny to be fulfilled. The accountability clause as individuals is a great place to start when deciding if we will embrace the journey of new beginnings.

Psalm 102:25 (NIV) In the beginning you laid the foundations of the earth, and the heavens are the work of your hands.

Lord, expand my thinking as you have extended your grace to me by considering me to travel a journey that was created by you for me.

**Today is a new day!**

Today I declare:

_____

_____

_____

_____

_____

_____

# DAY 25

As a believer it is foolishness to think prosperity only comes in the form of money. A carnal mind will think as such but those who believe the word of God understands otherwise.

Beloved, I pray that you may prosper in all things and be in health, just as your soul prospers. 3 John 1:2 (KJV)

Holy Spirit cover my thought process as I walk in prosperity in every area of my life

**Today is a new day!**

Today I declare:

_____

_____

_____

_____

_____

_____

# DAY 26

Apologizing for our obedience to God is like Him apologizing for saving us. I imagine those words penetrate so deep within us, causing us to refrain from going that route and repent if we have taken it.

Now, change your ways and what you are doing, and listen to the LORD your God. Then the LORD will change his plan about the disaster that he intends to bring on you. Jeremiah 26:13 (GWT)

Lord I repent and ask for forgiveness for allowing man to determine how I should be used instead of you. Forgive me for second guessing You and your instructions given to me as your vessel.

**Today is a new day!**

Today I declare:

_____

_____

_____

_____

_____

_____

# DAY 27

Be content in every season. Praise God while in wait. Thank Him for a season of growing.

Philippians 4:11-13 (ERV) I am telling you this, but not because I need something. I have learned to be satisfied with what I have and with whatever happens. I know how to live when I am poor and when I have plenty. I have learned the secret of how to live through any kind of situation when I have enough to eat or when I am hungry, when I have everything I need or when I have nothing. Christ is the one who gives me the strength I need to do whatever I must do.

Father thank you for every season I have experienced. Thank you for those seasons to come. Thank you for the season I am in, I trust you!

**Today is a new day!**

Today I declare:

_____

_____

_____

_____

_____

_____

# DAY 28

Your sense of self-worth should never be placed in the hands of man. Know your worth and who you are, not prideful, but confidently clothed with humility and purity in your heart.

Woe to those who are wise in their own eyes, and shrewd in their own sight Isaiah 5:21 (ESV)

Pray for those who have taken it upon themselves to sum you up according to their own assumptions. Repent if we have done the same in return

**Today is a new day!**

Today I declare:

_____

_____

_____

# DAY 29

Never make excuses for where God is taking you or refuse His counsel on any assignment. Make sure the buzz you hear from others does not over power the voice of God. This will cause you to become frustrated, making unsound and spontaneous decisions.

Without consultation, plans are frustrated, but with many counselors they succeed. Proverbs 15:22 (NASB)

Lord lead me every step of the way today as I inquire of you for my instructions

**Today is a new day!**

Today I declare:

_____

_____

_____

_____

_____

_____

# Day 30

We all have an opportunity to live successful lives when we put the Lord first. Living a life that is pleasing to Him...obedience is key.

Psalm 84:11 ( NIV ) For the LORD God is a sun and shield; the LORD bestows favor and honor; no good thing does he withhold from those whose walk is blameless.

Lord God, help me to walk in the steps you have already ordered for my life

**Today is a new day!**

## Today I declare:

_____

_____

_____

_____

_____

_____

# DAY 31

Hebrews 5: 11-14 (MSG) I have a lot more to say about this, but it is hard to get it across to you since you've picked up this bad habit of not listening. By this time you ought to be teachers yourselves, yet here I find you need someone to sit down with you and go over the basics on God again, starting from square one baby's milk, when you should have been on solid food long ago! Milk is for beginners, inexperienced in God's ways; solid food is for the mature, who have some practice in telling right from wrong.

Are we spoiled brats who continue to have "woe is me" pity parties or are we ready to be matured in the word. God wants us to come to an understanding that the world does not revolve around us. He desires for us to get to a place of understanding that as we grow lives are changed and souls are saved. He wants to know He can trust us to give Him all of us so we can be a catalyst i.e; impact in the earth. Are we still having temper tantrums when we cannot have our way or not being placed in the spotlight the way we think we should? Are we still quarreling and bickering, being a part of foolishness instead of pursuing what is on the heart of God. It's time for us to grow, so we can grow up in the Lord and teach others to do the same. Everyone is not at this place but some are, therefore we the mature must step up and step out as the Lord leads us so we will not have a generation of babies in Christ. No more re-crucifying Christ.

**Today is a new day!**

Today I declare:

_____

_____

_____

_____

_____

_____

Notes:

_____

_____

_____

_____

_____

_____

_____

_____

_____

_____

_____

_____

_____

_____

_____

_____

_____

_____

_____

_____

# ABOUT THE
# AUTHOR

Dr. Carolyn King-Robertson is a wife, the mother of four, grandmother of three but most of all a woman of God who understands without Him as head of her life, none of this is possible. Prophetess Carolyn is a inspirational speaker, author, mentor, children's youth director and host of His Heart Speaks Radio Broadcast and Co-Host of Let's Talk Real Talk Radio Broadcast.

Carolyn believes in speaking the unadulterated Word of God to bring about deliverance, healing and restoration to individuals from all walks of life while sharing the love of Jesus Christ to all the nations. She is the founder of No More Chain's In Christ Deliverance and Healing Ministry.

CAROLYN KING-ROBERTSON

www.ingramcontent.com/pod-product-compliance
Lightning Source LLC
Chambersburg PA
CBHW062027040426
42447CB00010B/2177